BASEBALL
RULES IN PICTURES

COLUMBUS BOOKS
LONDON

DEDICATION

To C. O. Brown, late president of the American Amateur Baseball Congress, who contributed his knowledge and advice to the preparation of this book as selflessly as he had devoted his life to amateur athletics on behalf of the youth of America.

Also gratefully acknowledged is the serving of George Barr, National League umpire for 20 years, and H. V. Porter, Former Executive Secretary of the National Federation of State High School Athletic Associations, as technical consultants.

Copyright © 1957, 1965, 1973, 1985 by A.G. Jacobs
Introduction © 1985 by Ron Luciano

First published in Great Britain in 1988 by
Columbus Books Limited
19-23 Ludgate Hill, London EC4M 7PD

British Library Cataloguing in Publication Data
McCrory, G. Jacobs
Baseball rules in pictures.
1. Baseball
I. Title II. McCrory, J.R.
796.357

ISBN 0–86287–413–0

Printed and bound by The Guernsey Press, Channel Islands

INTRODUCTION

The man, or woman, on the field in charge of a baseball game is called the umpire. Of course, if he makes a questionable call against the home team on a play, he will be called many other things too. I was a major league umpire for eleven years, and I always called the plays as I saw them—when I saw them. Players and managers often questioned my eyesight, my judgment, even my sanity, but they never questioned my knowledge of the rules.

An umpire has to know the rulebook. His job depends on it. I found during my career that those players and managers who really knew the rules were able to take full advantage of a situation on the field. I've seen teams lose games because a player left a base earlier than permitted, or because a pitcher didn't realize he was committing a balk. And, in 1914, a team actually lost the pennant because a runner did not know he had to touch second base when the batter hit a single and a runner on third base scored the "winning" run.

The basic rules of baseball are not complicated. Perhaps the simplest explanation of the rules I have ever heard came from the grandmother of a childhood friend of mine. "One man throws the ball at another man," she said. "The other man tries to hit it with a stick. If he is able to hit it, he is so happy that he runs around like a crazy person!"

Actually, she almost had it right. Baseball is a game of throwing, hitting, catching, and running. And once you have mastered those skills, you will be able to play the game on any level. But as important as it is to be able to do those things, you must know the rules of the game.

When I was growing up in Endicott, New York, we had to make rules that conformed to our ballfield. If a ball rolled down a water-grate the batter was entitled to a double. If a ball went rolling down the hill, the last one down—the last player to get on his knees—had to get it. And finally, if it went anywhere near Biondo's Bakery, the place with the sweetest rolls and most delicious cakes I've ever tasted, I was not allowed to retrieve it.

But as I got older, and baseball fields became a little more uniform, I learned that a single set of rules governs all organized baseball. I liked that—unlike math, a subject in which every time I thought I'd learned it, they would add another rule or complication.

Knowing the rules will not help you hit a pitch farther or enable you to throw a better fastball. What it will do is to give you the same opportunity to win as the most knowledgeable player on the field. The player who doesn't know the rules starts with a disadvantage that sometimes even talent isn't enough to overcome.

I think baseball is the most beautiful game there is to watch, and one of the most enjoyable to play. But to play it right, you have to know the game inside and out. So remember, learn the rules, keep your eye on the baseball, and please, please, never, ever argue with the umpire.

He's trying just as hard as you are—and he may be my relative.

Ron Luciano

FOREWORD

Baseball is the all-American ballgame with which millions of non-Americans are becoming familiar through the small screen. In Britain, baseball was first televised on a regular basis in January 1986, and Channel 4 plans to make the World Series (October each year) a major fixture in the British TV viewer's sporting calendar.

Here is the book all TV baseball fans need to enable them to follow the game and get the most enjoyment from it. It's a quick and easy way to learn the rules and check on any questions arising from them.

The plan of the book is simplicity itself. Nearly 200 clear pictures illustrate actual playing situations and the captions explain the rules involved. For those who want to check the wording of the rule itself, every caption is keyed to the Official Baseball Rules in the back of the book. The book is divided into four parts: The Pitcher, The Batter, The Runner, The Umpire. The selection from the Official Baseball Rules covers those rules that apply to all organized leagues with exceptions for Little Leagues noted. Matters of organization, equipment and the playing field are not covered since they vary among amateur leagues.

The pictures and captions are taken from an educational film strip prepared by Teaching Aids Service, Inc., which has been praised by teachers, coaches, professional umpires, and amateur league officials throughout the USA.

Part 1:
THE PITCHER

To begin play the umpire calls "Play!" while the pitcher is in the pitching position. (Rule 4.02)

SET POSITION

WIND UP POSITION

The pitcher may use one of two starting positions. Either is legal at any time. (Rule 8.01 a-b)

WIND UP POSITION

The pitcher must stand squarely facing the batter, with his pivot foot **ON** or **IN FRONT** of the pitcher's plate. (Rule 8.01 a)

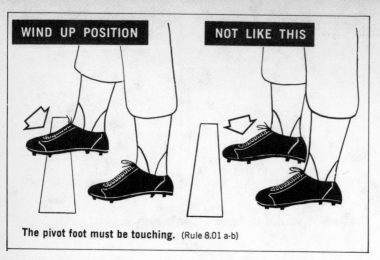

WIND UP POSITION   **NOT LIKE THIS**

The pivot foot must be touching. (Rule 8.01 a-b)

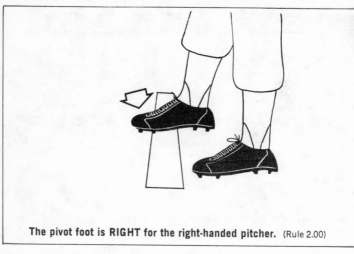

The pivot foot is RIGHT for the right-handed pitcher. (Rule 2.00)

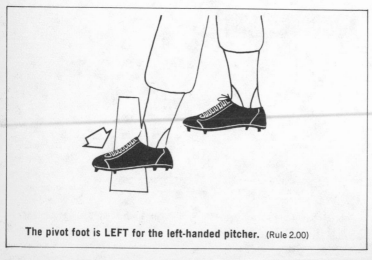

The pivot foot is LEFT for the left-handed pitcher. (Rule 2.00)

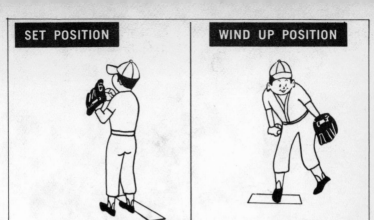

SET POSITION

WIND UP POSITION

The pitcher's pivot foot must touch the rubber in either position.
(Rule 8.01 a-b)

WIND UP POSITION

His other foot is free, but the pitcher must not raise either foot from the ground except to deliver the ball. (Rule 8.01 a)

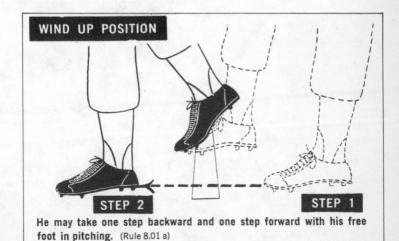

WIND UP POSITION

STEP 2

STEP 1

He may take one step backward and one step forward with his free foot in pitching. (Rule 8.01 a)

9

In the set position the pitcher faces the batter sideways
with ENTIRE pivot foot ON or IN FRONT OF and IN CONTACT
with the rubber. (Rule 8.01 b)

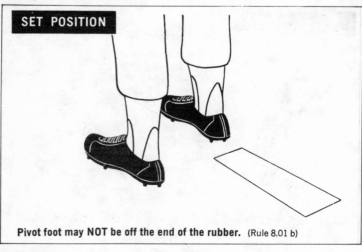

SET POSITION

Pivot foot may NOT be off the end of the rubber. (Rule 8.01 b)

STARTING POSITION

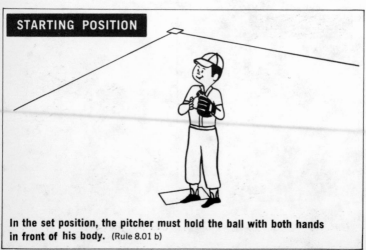

In the set position, the pitcher must hold the ball with both hands
in front of his body. (Rule 8.01 b)

SET POSITION

He may stretch and return, but must come to a complete stop before pitching. (Rule 8.01 b)

NOTE: The rules concerning a pitcher's throw to a base to catch a runner do not apply in Little League play, since the Little League rules require all runners to remain on base until the pitch has reached the batter..

SET POSITION.

After taking the SET position, the pitcher may pitch to the batter—or (Rule 8.01 b)

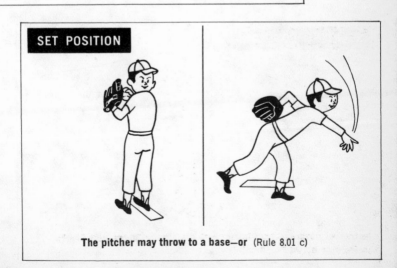

SET POSITION

The pitcher may throw to a base—or (Rule 8.01 c)

FROM THE SET POSITION

The pitcher may step backward off rubber with pivot foot before "breaking" hands for actual pitch to batter or throw to base. (Rule 8.01 b)

If a pitcher throws to base, he must step directly toward that base.
Penalty: Balk. (Rule 8.01 c)

With no runner on base, pitcher must deliver ball within 20 seconds after receiving it. Penalty: Umpire calls "Ball" for each violation. This does not apply in Little League. (Rule 8.04)

He may not deface the ball in any way before pitching.
Penalty: Eviction from game. (Rule 8.02 a; 3.02)

If there is a runner or runners, the pitcher, while touching his plate, may not throw, or feint a throw, to an unoccupied base, except for the purpose of making a play. Penalty: Balk (Rule 8.05 d)

The pitcher may not intentionally pitch at the batter.
Penalty: Eviction from the game after a warning. (Rule 8.02 d)

A BALK

A balk is an act by a pitcher to unfairly take advantage of; or to deceive, a runner. A balk pitch is not a ball or strike. (Penalty: If ball is not hit, award all runners one base advance.) A balk is not an appeal play. Umpire must call it immediately upon commission.

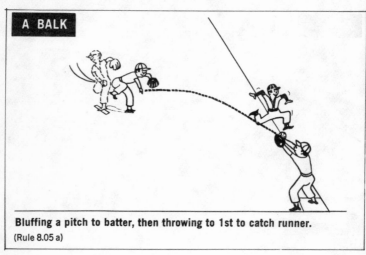

A BALK

Bluffing a pitch to batter, then throwing to 1st to catch runner. (Rule 8.05 a)

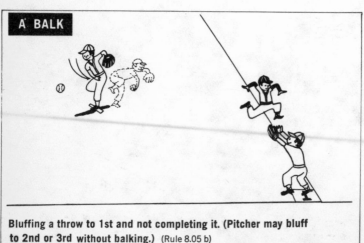

A BALK

Bluffing a throw to 1st and not completing it. (Pitcher may bluff to 2nd or 3rd without balking.) (Rule 8.05 b)

A BALK

Pitcher making a motion associated with pitching to batter and failing to complete pitch. (Rule 8.05 a)

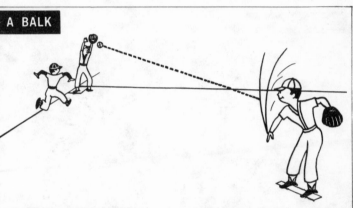

A BALK

Throwing to any base to catch a runner without stepping directly toward that base. (Rule 8.05 c)

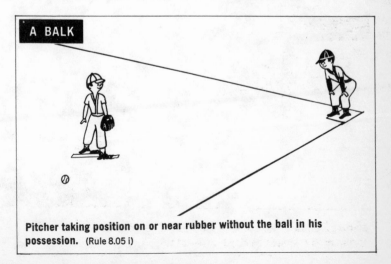

A BALK

Pitcher taking position on or near rubber without the ball in his possession. (Rule 8.05 i)

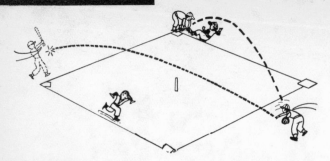

NO. 1 FOR ALL BALKS

Penalty—if ball is hit fairly. When batter and runners advance at least one base safely—play stands—even if any runner is put out trying to advance further. (Rule 8.05)

NO. 2 FOR ALL BALKS

Go back!

Penalty—if ball is hit fairly. When batter and runners **DO NOT** advance at least one base safely—runners are given one base from original base held at balk.   Batter returns to bat. (Rule 8.05)

A QUICK QUIZ

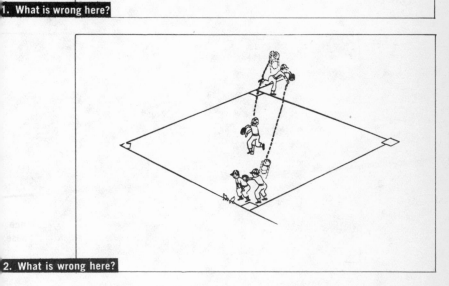

1. What is wrong here?

2. What is wrong here?

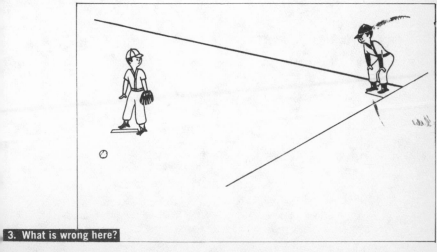

3. What is wrong here?

17

1. The pitcher did not step toward 1st base as he threw the ball.
   (Rule 8.01 c)

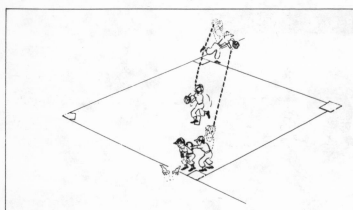

2. Pitcher threw to unoccupied base, but not to make the play there.
   (Rule 8.05 d)

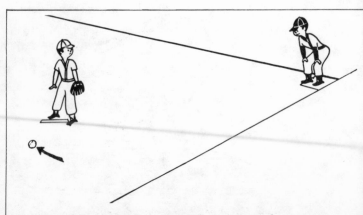

3. The pitcher does not have the ball and the pivot foot is not touching the rubber. (Rule 8.05 i)

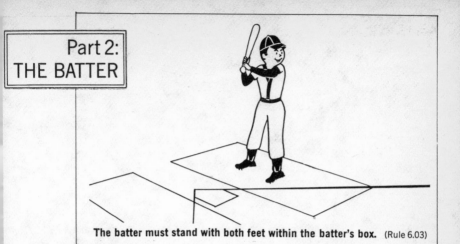

Part 2: THE BATTER

The batter must stand with both feet within the batter's box. (Rule 6.03)

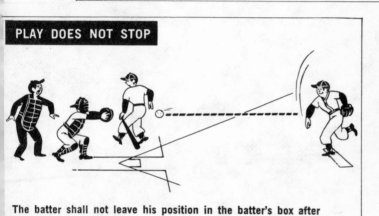

The batter shall not leave his position in the batter's box after the pitcher comes to the "Set" position or starts his windup.
Penalty: "Ball" or "Strike" as the case may be. (Rule 6.02 b)

He is OUT if he hits the ball with either foot entirely outside lines of batter's box. (Rule 6.06 a and Rule 2.00 ILLEGALLY BATTED BALL.)

Any ball at which he swings and misses is a STRIKE, regardless of position of pitch. (Rule 2.00)

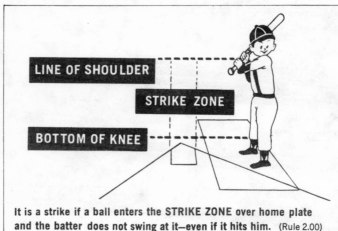

It is a strike if a ball enters the STRIKE ZONE over home plate and the batter does not swing at it—even if it hits him. (Rule 2.00)

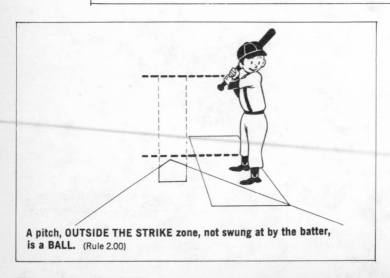

A pitch, OUTSIDE THE STRIKE zone, not swung at by the batter, is a BALL. (Rule 2.00)

FAIR BALL

A fair ball must:

1. Settle in fair territory between first and third bases—or
2. Bounce past third or first base in fair territory—or
3. Bounce over first or third base—or
4. Fall fair and roll foul beyond first or third base
5. Be over fair territory when it passes out of playing field in flight

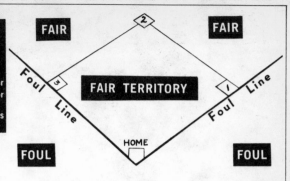

FAIR | FAIR

FAIR TERRITORY

Foul Line | Foul Line

HOME

FOUL | FOUL

FAIR territory is territory within foul lines. FOUL territory is area outside the foul lines. (Rule 2.00)

THE RUNNER IS CALLED BACK

THE BALL IS DEAD

It is a fair ball if it strikes the umpire on fair territory—before touching a fielder or passing a fielder other than the pitcher. (Rule 2.00; 6.08 d)

THE BALL IS DEAD

It is a fair ball if it strikes a player on fair territory. Runner struck is out. Batter goes to first; others advance **ONLY** if forced. (Rule 2.00; 6.08 d)

A foul direct off the bat to the catcher and caught is a **FOUL TIP** and is in play. If caught on rebound, **NOT A CATCH** unless ball touches catcher's glove or hand first. (Rule 2.00)

A batter may run when he hits a fair ball. (Rule 6.09 a)

A batter may run when he has three strikes—if the catcher fails to catch the ball, unless first base is occupied and there are less than 2 outs. This does not apply to Little Leagues. (Rule 6.09 b)

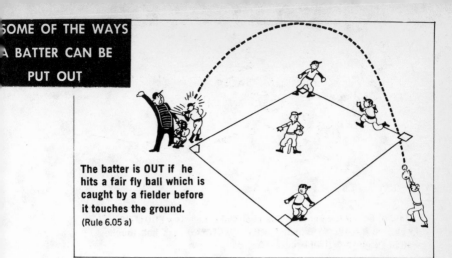

The batter is OUT if he hits a fair fly ball which is caught by a fielder before it touches the ground. (Rule 6.05 a)

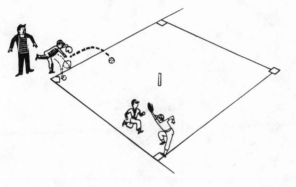

The batter is out if he hits a foul fly ball which is caught by a fielder before it touches the ground. (Rule 6.05 a)

The batter is out if his third strike is caught by the catcher. (Rule 6.05 b)

The batter is also out after third strike not caught if less than two are out and a runner is on 1st. (Rule 6.05 c)

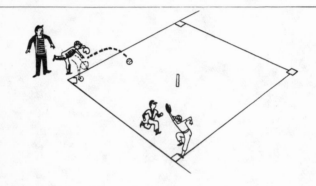

If the 3rd strike is not caught—with less than 2 out and 1st base is not occupied —the runner is safe if he can beat the throw to 1st. This does not apply to Little League. (Rule 6.09 b)

INFIELD FLY

An infield fly is a fair fly ball which can reasonably be handled by an infielder and which occurs when there are fewer than two outs and there are runners on first and second, whether or not there may also be a runner on third.

The umpire should call, "Infield fly; batter out if fair."

Runners advance at their own risk.

The batter is OUT on an infield fly; but a runner on his base struck by an infield fly is NOT OUT. (Rule 7.08 f)

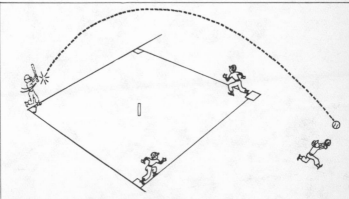

"Rule of thumb" to determine if infield fly: Could fielder be facing toward batter when making catch? Here NOT an infield fly. (Rule 2.00)

The batter is out if he bunts the third strike foul. (Rule 6.05 d)

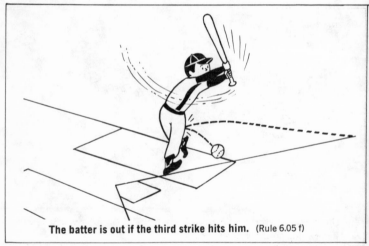

The batter is out if the third strike hits him. (Rule 6.05 f)

The batter is out if his fair hit ball bounces up and hits him before touching a fielder. (Rule 6.05 g)

The batter is out if the ball is held by a fielder on 1st base after a third strike —not caught. (Rule 6.05 j)

The batter is out if a fair hit ball is held by a fielder on first base before the batter reaches 1st. (Rule 6.05 j)

The batter is OUT if touched before he reaches 1st base on a fair hit ball, or on a 3rd strike which is not caught. (Rule 6.05 j)

THE BALL REMAINS IN PLAY

The batter is NOT out if he drops the bat and the ball rolls and hits the bat, unless the umpire judges act as intentional. (Rule 6.05 h)

The batter is out if he runs more than 3 feet out of the baseline to avoid being tagged. (Rule 7.08 a)

The batter is out if he interferes with a fielder. (Rule 6.05 k; 7.08 b)

A force out is made by tagging a base ahead of a runner only when he is forced to advance because batter becomes a runner. (Rule 7.08 e)

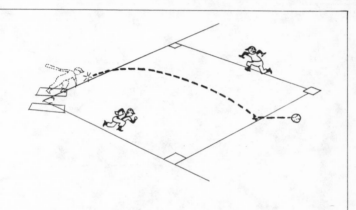

This situation is not a force play. First base is open for the batter. (Rule 7.08 e)

Unless a force play, no runner can force another runner. He retains right to base. Man originally on 1st base must get back. (Rule 7.03)

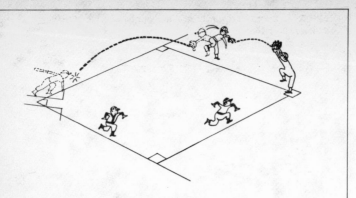

The batter is out when an infielder intentionally drops a fly ball (to make a force play possible). (Rule 6.05 l)

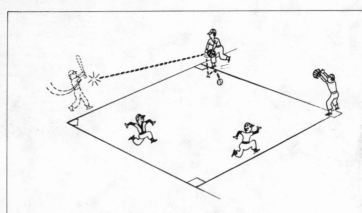

A batter is out when an infielder intentionally drops a line drive (in order to make a force play possible). (Rule 6.05 l)

THE BALL IS DEAD

The batter is out when a runner interferes with a defensive player catching a thrown ball, or throwing to complete a play.
Additional Penalty: Runners return. (Rule 6.05 m)

The batter is out when a spectator clearly prevents a fielder from catching a fly ball.
(Rule 3.16 APPROVED RULING)

The legal batter is out if someone else bats in his turn. Improper batter is not out. Appeal must be made to umpire by defensive team before the next play or attempted play. If not so appealed the play stands. Under High School rules, the scorer, umpire, or any offensive player may correct the infraction without penalty before the ball is pitched to improper batter.

The proper batter Number 2 comes to bat and assumes the ball and strike count of the improper batter Number 3. (Rule 6.07)

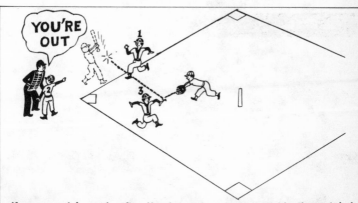

If an appeal is made after Number 3 has completed his time at bat and before the next pitch to batter, the next play or attempted play, Number 2 is out. Bases run and scores do not count. (Rule 6.07 b)

31

"Jeopardy" means in danger of being put out, as the ball is in play.

To be "awarded" a base means to be permitted to advance there without jeopardy—that is, without danger of being put out.

The batter is awarded 1st base by having 4 balls called by the umpire. (Rule 6.08 a)

The batter is awarded 1st base if catcher or any other fielder interferes with him unless his manager notifies umpire immediately that he wishes play to stand because it is to his advantage. (Rule 6.08 c)

THE BALL IS DEAD

The batter is awarded 1st base when a fair hit ball strikes
the umpire before touching or passing a fielder,
other than the pitcher. (Rule 6.08 d)

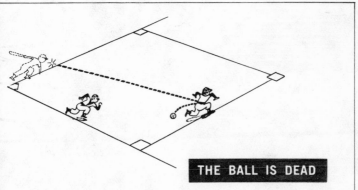

THE BALL IS DEAD

The batter is awarded 1st base when his fair hit ball strikes the runner
before touching or passing a fielder, other than the pitcher.
Runner is out. (Rule 6.08d; 7.08 f)

THE BALL IS DEAD

The batter is awarded 1st base if struck by a pitched ball not in the strike
zone which he is not attempting to hit and which he tries to avoid.
(Rule 6.08 b)

If the batter does not try to avoid a pitched ball it is called ball or strike as the case may be. (Note to Rule 6.08 b)

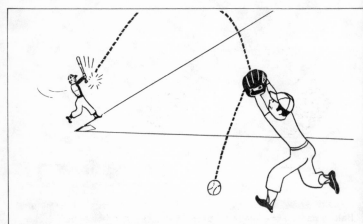

The ball is dead on a foul fly not caught. Runners return. (Rule 5.09 e)

The ball is dead when a thrown ball or a fair hit ball goes into the stands. Runners advance. (Rule 7.05)

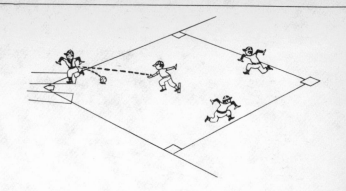

The ball is dead if a legally pitched ball hits a runner trying to score. Runners advance. (Rule 5.09 h)

Ball is dead if the umpire interferes with a catcher attempting to throw to catch runner. Runners return. (Rule 5.09 b)

DEAD BALL

When the ball is dead the play stops. No runs count and no one can advance—
   except as the result of acts while the ball was alive.
The most common exceptions are:

EXCEPTION 1

Overthrow into crowd. (Rule 7.05 g-h)

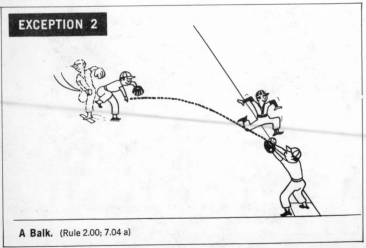

EXCEPTION 2

A Balk. (Rule 2.00; 7.04 a)

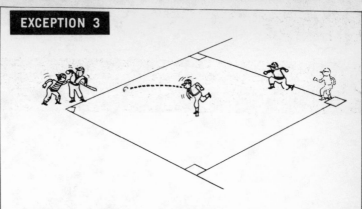

EXCEPTION 3

SOMETIMES on Obstruction or Interference, but only under circumstances described in these pictures.

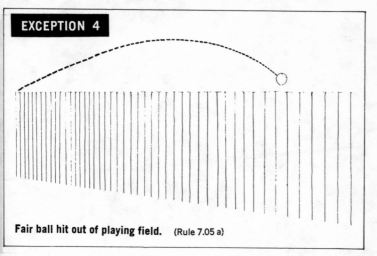

EXCEPTION 4

Fair ball hit out of playing field. (Rule 7.05 a)

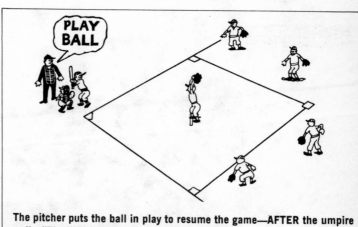

The pitcher puts the ball in play to resume the game—AFTER the umpire calls "Play!" The ball is now in play. (Rule 5.11)

A QUICK QUIZ

1. Is this bunt FAIR or FOUL?

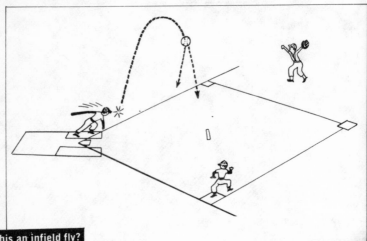

2. Why isn't this an infield fly?

3. Why is the runner out?

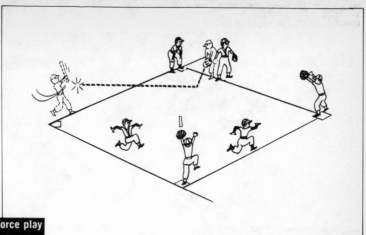

4. Where is a force play possible?

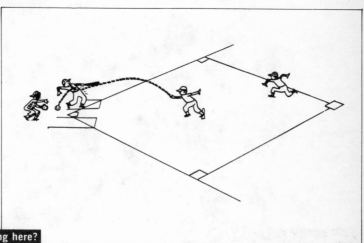

5. What is wrong here?

6. What do you do with the runners here?

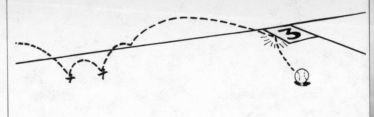

1. **FAIR. It came back by 3rd base.** (Rule 2.00)

2. **Runner on first only when ball was hit.** (Rule 2.00)

3. **The runner ran more than 3 feet out of the baseline to avoid being tagged.** (Rule 7.08 a)

4. 2nd and 1st only. Runner on third not forced. (Rule 7.08 e)

5. Ball is dead. Runner on 2nd does not advance. (Rule 5.09 a)

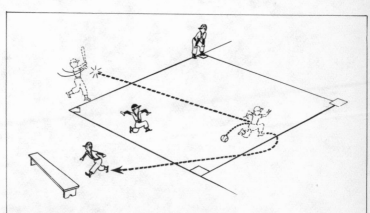

6. Award batter 1st. Runner hit is out. Runner on 3rd does not advance—not forced to do so. (Rule 5.09 f; 7.08 f)

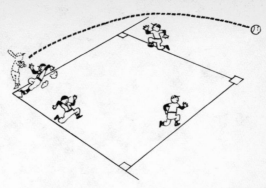

Part 3:
THE RUNNER

The runner must touch 1st, 2nd, 3rd and home bases in order to score a run. (Rule 2.00; 7.02)

If forced to return, a runner must touch bases in reverse order— unless the ball is dead. (Rule 7.02)

Two runners may not occupy the same base. The first runner retains right to base, except on a force play. (Rule 7.01)

If not a force play, and a following runner is tagged while on base, he is out. (Rule 7.03)

RUNNER ADVANCES

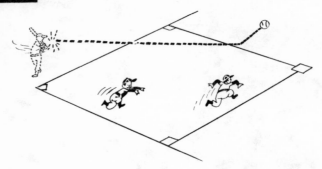

Runners advance one base without jeopardy when batter is awarded 1st base and runners must advance to open base for him. (Rule 7.04 b)

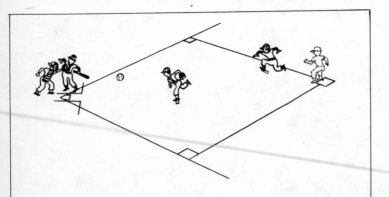

The runner is entitled to advance without jeopardy to base he is attempting to steal if catcher interferes with batter. (Rule 7.04 d)

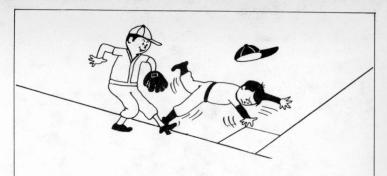

If play is made on runner obstructed by a defensive player, ball is dead and he must be awarded at least one base. (Rule 7.06 a)
If no play is made on obstructed runner, play goes to completion and umpire imposes penalties, if necessary, to nullify obstruction. (Rule 7.06 b)

All runners and batter are entitled to advance home without jeopardy when a fair ball is hit over the fence. (Rule 7.05 a)

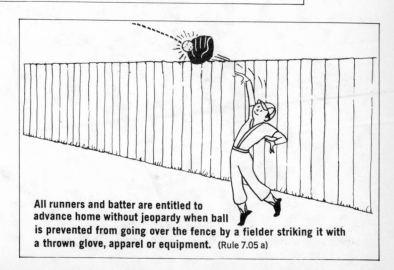

All runners and batter are entitled to advance home without jeopardy when ball is prevented from going over the fence by a fielder striking it with a thrown glove, apparel or equipment. (Rule 7.05 a)

THE HIGH SCHOOL RULES DISCOURAGE THIS

All runners and batter advance 3 bases without jeopardy if a fielder touches any fair ball with a thrown mask, glove or detached part of uniform. **Batter** may try for home at his own risk. (Rule 7.05 b)

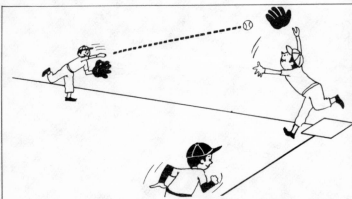

If a ball is thrown, not batted, and a fielder strikes it with a thrown glove or any other piece of equipment, runners and the batter advance 2 bases without jeopardy—more at own risk. (Rule 7.05 e)

The runner is awarded 2 bases, without jeopardy, from base occupied at time ball was pitched, if throw was first by an infielder unless runners had advanced at least one base at time throw was made. (Rule 7.05 g)

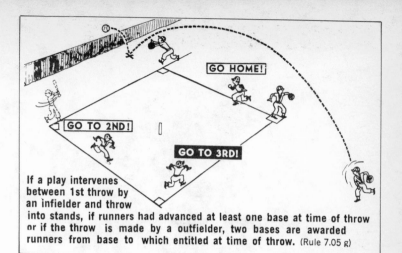

GO HOME!

GO TO 2ND!

GO TO 3RD!

If a play intervenes between 1st throw by an infielder and throw into stands, if runners had advanced at least one base at time of throw or if the throw is made by a outfielder, two bases are awarded runners from base to which entitled at time of throw. (Rule 7.05 g)

A wild pitch to batter which goes into the stands, bench, etc., entitles runners to advance one base without jeopardy. (Rule 7.05 h)

When the runner on 3rd attempts to score on steal or squeeze bunt and catcher interferes with batter, award runner home, batter 1st. (Rule 7.07)

The runner is out when he fails to yield right of way to a fielder fielding a fair hit ball. (Rule 7.08 b)

The runner is out when he intentionally interferes with a thrown ball. (Rule 7.08 b)

The runner is out when he is tagged by a fielder while off base. (Rule 7.08 c)

The runner is out if he passes the preceding runner unless that runner has been put out as occurs occasionally on "run-down" plays. (Rule 7.08 h)

The runner is out when the base to which he is advancing on a force play is tagged. (Rule 7.08 e)

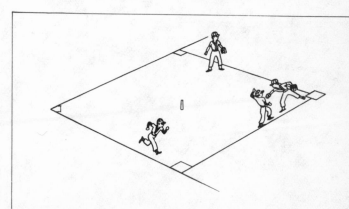

A runner is out when he is tagged with the ball on a force play. (Rule 7.08 e)

APPEAL PLAYS

An appeal must be made to the umpire by a defensive player before the next pitch to the batter, the next play or attempted play such as trying to catch a runner off base. (Rule 7.10)

An appeal is defined by the rules as the act of a fielder in claiming a violation of the rules by the offensive team. (Rule 2.00)

Hitting with an illegal bat (such as a loaded or deliberately flattened bat) is now an appeal play and batter is out on proper appeal after he hits with such a bat. (Rule 6.06 d and Rule 2.00 ILLEGALLY BATTED BALL.)

THIS IS AN APPEAL PLAY

If a runner leaves base before a fly ball, fair or foul, is caught, he is out if the base is tagged before his return to base. (Rule 7.08 d)

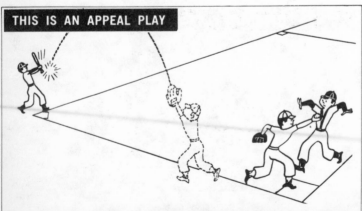

THIS IS AN APPEAL PLAY

If a runner leaves base before a fly ball, fair or foul, is caught, he is out if he is tagged before his return to base. (Rule 7.08 d)

THIS IS AN APPEAL PLAY

If a runner misses a base, he may be put out by a fielder touching the base with the ball before the runner retags the base. (Rule 7.10 b)

THIS IS AN APPEAL PLAY

Failing to return to 1st base immediately after overrunning or oversliding. (Rule 7.10 c)

THIS IS AN APPEAL PLAY

The runner is out if he overslides home plate—misses it—and the plate is tagged by a fielder before the runner returns. (Rule 7.10 d)

A baserunner must return to base on a foul ball not caught. Umpire shall not put ball in play until all runners have retouched their bases. (Rule 5.09 e)

The runner need not retouch after a foul tip as this is considered a regular strike. (Rule 2.00)

INTERFERENCE PLAYS

On all interference plays the ball is dead and runner returns to base occupied when ball was pitched.

INTERFERENCE

THE BALL IS DEAD. RUNNERS RETURN TO BASE

The batter interferes with play at plate. If less than 2 outs—the runner is out. If 2 are out—the batter is out. (Rule 7.08 g)

INTERFERENCE

THE BALL IS DEAD. RUNNERS RETURN TO BASE

The runner is out, if on third, and the coach leaves the coach's box to make movement intended to draw the throw from the fielder. (Rule 7.09 j)

The runner is out if teammates gather around a base to which runner is advancing to confuse or hinder the defensive team. (Rule 7.09 e)

THESE RUNS SCORE

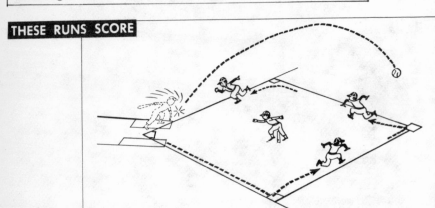

If a preceding runner "misses" a base, it does not affect the baserunners behind him, whether put out or not, unless it's the 3rd out. (Rule 7.12)

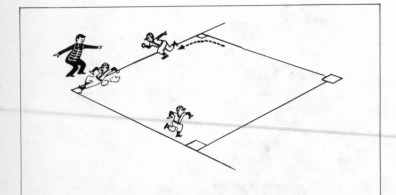

Runs score if appeal play for third out is behind runner unless it is a force out. (Rule 7.12)

If the batter is put out before reaching 1st. (Rule 4.09 a)

If any other runner is put out by a force out for 3rd out. (Rule 4.09 a)

If a preceding runner is the 3rd out on an appeal play. (Rule 4.09 a)

A QUICK QUIZ

1. Where do you place the players?

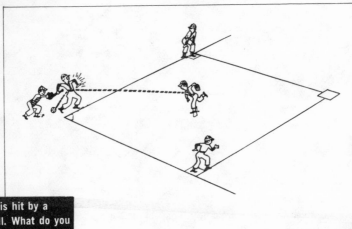

2. The batter is hit by a pitched ball. What do you do with the runners?

3. What is your decision?

What are baserunning appeal plays?

Does the second run count?

What is your decision?

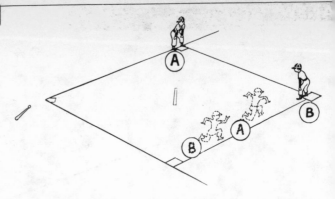

1. Place runner on 3rd and 2nd. One cannot put two men on one base
(CASEBOOK 7.05 g)

**2. Advance runner on 1st to 2nd. Put batter on 1st.
Hold runner on 3rd.** (Rule 7.04 b)

**3. Wait until end of play since no play is made on obstructed runner
Then impose penalties to nullify act of obstruction,
if necessary.** (Rule 7.06)

THIS IS AN APPEAL PLAY

4-a. Missing a base. (Rule 7.10 b)

THIS IS AN APPEAL PLAY

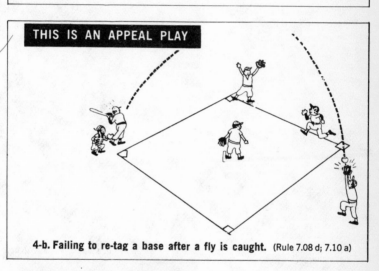

4-b. Failing to re-tag a base after a fly is caught. (Rule 7.08 d; 7.10 a)

THIS IS AN APPEAL PLAY

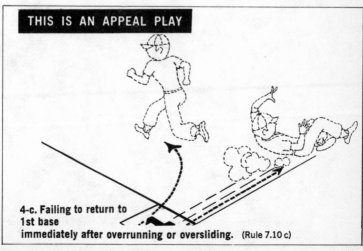

4-c. Failing to return to 1st base immediately after overrunning or oversliding. (Rule 7.10 c)

THIS IS AN APPEAL PLAY

4-d. Missing home plate. (Rule 7.10 d)

5. NO. The run does **NOT** count if the appeal is third out. (Rule 4.09 a)

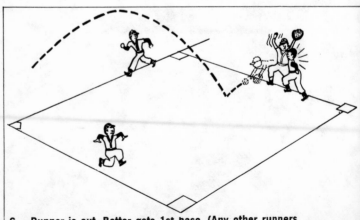

6. Runner is out. Batter gets 1st base. (Any other runners return to base.) (Rule 7.08 b)

Part 4:
THE UMPIRE

ome Duties of the Umpire
efore the Game.

See that the field is marked plainly. (Rule 3.01 b)

To be a good umpire is something to be proud of. It is not an easy job, but there is great satisfaction from doing it right. Of course you must know the game and you must keep alert; but beyond that you must be careful to keep your feelings in complete control. "Call the plays, never the players."

See that pitcher's rubber is in good condition. (Rule 3.01 a)

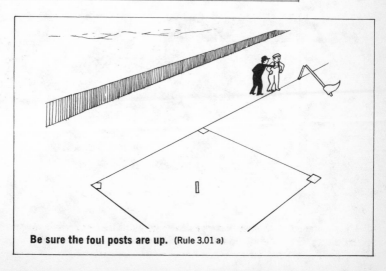

Be sure the foul posts are up. (Rule 3.01 a)

Receive batting orders in duplicate. Check to be sure they are identical.
Give extra copy to opposing manager. (Rule 4.01 a-c)

NATIONAL LEAGUE'S STYLE — UMPIRE JUDGES BALLS AND STRIKES OVER CATCHER'S SHOULDER NEAREST BATTER

Be in a position to call all plays. If working alone, start game
behind the plate.

KEEP YOUR EYE ON THE BALL   **HUSTLE**

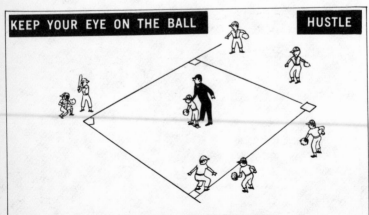

With a runner on 1st only, take position behind pitcher.
Try not to '"shadow" the pitch to batter.

When there is one umpire, he remains behind the plate when there are runners on bases other than first.

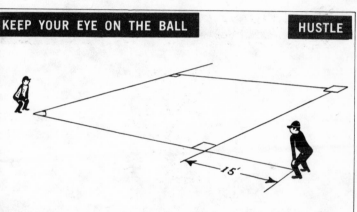

KEEP YOUR EYE ON THE BALL   HUSTLE

15'

Most Amateur games use two umpires. One is always behind the plate. With nobody on base, the other umpire stands as shown.

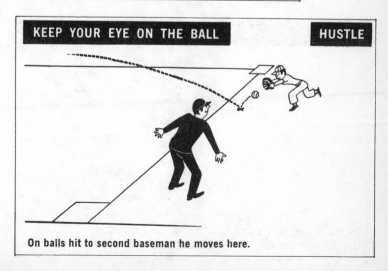

KEEP YOUR EYE ON THE BALL   HUSTLE

On balls hit to second baseman he moves here.

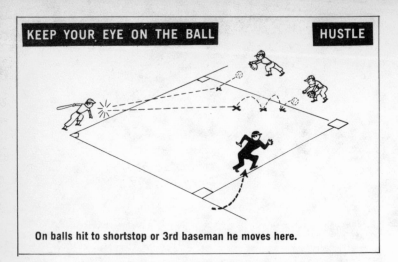

KEEP YOUR EYE ON THE BALL　　　　HUSTLE

On balls hit to shortstop or 3rd baseman he moves here.

BE IN A POSITION TO SEE EVERY PLAY

On other than tag plays, "Listen" for ball in glove, "Look" for tag of runner's foot and also try to catch ball out of the corner of your eye.

KEEP YOUR EYE ON THE BALL　　　　HUSTLE

With runner on second, stand (R) for right-handed pitchers, (L) for left-handed pitchers to prevent "shadowing" the ball.

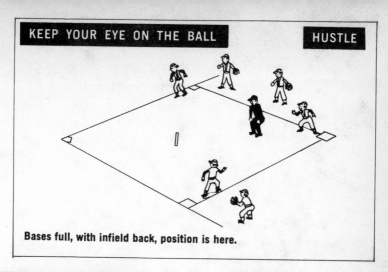

Bases full, with infield back, position is here.

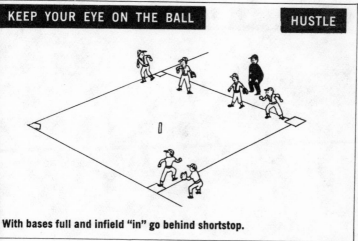

With bases full and infield "in" go behind shortstop.

With runner on third only, one or none out, many umpires prefer this position.

The umpire's signal for a strike.

THE MOST COMMON SIGNALS

KEEP YOUR EYE ON THE BALL

The umpire's signal for out.

KEEP YOUR EYE ON THE BALL

HUSTLE

The signal for safe.

BE IN A POSITION TO SEE EVERY PLAY

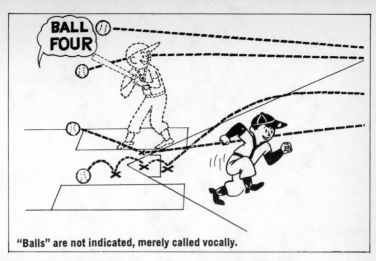

"Balls" are not indicated, merely called vocally.

Call FOUL balls only when sure and when ball will be close.
Do not call FAIR balls.
Indicate by pointing whether ball is INSIDE or OUTSIDE the foul line.

Give balls on left hand, strikes on right every few pitches.
It avoids unnecessary questions.

Don't "give away" appeal plays.

KEEP YOUR EYE ON THE BALL

Be in a position to see every play.

Don't call plays on the run. Set yourself.

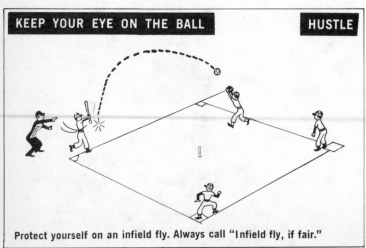

KEEP YOUR EYE ON THE BALL　　　**HUSTLE**

Protect yourself on an infield fly. Always call "Infield fly, if fair."

To avoid arguments between innings, walk slightly from home plate toward bench of team going into field.

HUSTLE

When anyone argues, listen briefly, say "I saw the play this way and that's it. Play ball." Then walk a few steps away.

KEEP YOUR EYE ON THE BALL

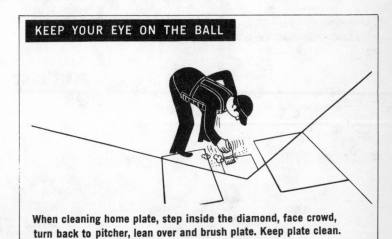

When cleaning home plate, step inside the diamond, face crowd, turn back to pitcher, lean over and brush plate. Keep plate clean.

2.00—Definitions of Terms.

(All definitions in Rule 2.00 are listed alphabetically.)

ADJUDGED is a judgment decision by the umpire.

An APPEAL is the act of a fielder in claiming violation of the rules by the offensive team.

A BALK is an illegal act by the pitcher with a runner or runners on base, entitling all runners to advance one base.

A BALL is a pitch which does not enter the strike zone in flight and is not struck at by the batter.

If the pitch touches the ground and bounces through the strike zone it is a "ball." If such a pitch touches the batter, he shall be awarded first base. If the batter swings at such a pitch after two strikes, the ball cannot be caught, for the purposes of Rule 6.05 (c) and 6.09 (b). If the batter hits such a pitch, the ensuing action shall be the same as if he hit the ball in flight.

A BASE is one of four points which must be touched by a runner in order to score a run; more usually applied to the canvas bags and the rubber plate which mark the base points.

A BASE COACH is a team member in uniform who is stationed in the coach's box at first or third base to direct the batter and the runners.

A BASE ON BALLS is an award of first base granted to a batter who, during his time at bat, receives four pitches outside the strike zone.

A BATTER is an offensive player who takes his position in the batter's box.

BATTER-RUNNER is a term that identifies the offensive player who has just finished his time at bat until he is put out or until the play on which he became a runner ends.

The BATTER'S BOX is the area within which the batter shall stand during his time at bat.

The BATTERY is the pitcher and catcher.

BENCH OR DUGOUT is the seating facilities reserved for players, substitutes and other team members in uniform when they are not actively engaged on the playing field.

A BUNT is a batted ball not swung at, but intentionally met with the bat and tapped slowly within the infield.

A CALLED GAME is one in which, for any reason, the umpire-in-chief terminates play.

A CATCH is the act of a fielder in getting secure possession in his hand or glove of a ball in flight and firmly holding it; providing he does not use his cap, protector, pocket or any other part of his uniform in getting possession. It is not a catch, however, if simultaneously or immediately following his contact with the ball, he collides with a player, or with a wall, or if he falls down, and as a result of such collision or falling, drops the ball. It is not a catch if a fielder touches a fly ball which then hits a member of the offensive team or an umpire and then is caught by another defensive player. If the fielder has made the catch and drops the ball while in the act of making a throw following the catch, the ball shall be adjudged to have been caught. In establishing the validity of the catch, the fielder shall hold the ball long enough to prove that he has complete control of the ball and that his release of the ball is voluntary and intentional.

A catch is legal if the ball is finally held by any fielder, even though juggled, or held by another fielder before it touches the ground. Runners may leave their bases the instant the first fielder touches the ball. A fielder may reach over a fence, railing, rope or other line of demarcation to make a catch. He may jump on top of a railing, or canvas that may be in foul ground. No interference should be allowed when a fielder reaches over a fence, railing, rope or into a stand to catch a ball. He does so at his own risk.

If a fielder, attempting a catch at the edge of the dugout, is "held up" and kept from an apparent fall by a player or players of either team and the catch is made, it shall be allowed.

The CATCHER is the fielder who takes his position back of the home base.

The CATCHER'S BOX is that area within which the catcher shall stand until the pitcher delivers the ball.

THE CLUB is a person or group of persons responsible for assembling the team personnel, providing the playing field and required facilities, and representing the team in relations with the league.

A COACH is a team member in uniform appointed by the manager to perform such duties as the manager may designate, such as but not limited to acting as base coach.

A DEAD BALL is a ball out of play because of a legally created temporary suspension of play.

The DEFENSE (or DEFENSIVE) is the team, or any player of the team, in the field.

A DOUBLE-HEADER is two regularly scheduled or rescheduled games, played in immediate succession.

A DOUBLE PLAY is a play by the defense in which two offensive players are put out as a result of continuous action, providing there is no error between putouts.

(a) A force double play is one in which both putouts are force plays.

(b) A reverse force double play is one in which the first out is a force play and the second out is made on a runner for whom

the force is removed by reason of the first out. Examples reverse force plays: runner on first, one out; batter grounds first baseman, who steps on first base (one out) and throws second baseman or shortstop for the second out (a tag play)

Another example: bases loaded, none out; batter grounds third baseman, who steps on third base (one out), then throws to catcher for the second out (tag play).

DUGOUT (See definition of BENCH)

A FAIR BALL is a batted ball that settles on fair ground between home and first base, or between home and third base, or that is on over fair territory when bounding to the outfield past first or third base, or that touches first, second or third base, or that first falls fair territory on or beyond first base or third base, or that, while on over fair territory, touches the person of an umpire or player, or tha while over fair territory, passes out of the playing field in flight.

A fair fly shall be judged according to the relative position of the ball and the foul line, including the foul pole, and not as to whether the fielder is on fair or foul territory at the time he touches the ball.

If a fly ball lands in the infield between home and first base, or home a third base, and then bounces to foul territory without touching a player umpire and before passing first or third base, it is a foul ball; or if the ba settles on foul territory or is touched by a player on foul territory, it is a fo ball. If a fly ball lands on or beyond first or third base and then bounces foul territory, it is a fair hit.

Clubs, increasingly, are erecting tall foul poles at the fence line with wire netting extending along the side of the pole on fair territory above t fence to enable the umpires more accurately to judge fair and foul balls.

FAIR TERRITORY is that part of the playing field within, a including the first base and third base lines, from home base to t bottom of the playing field fence and perpendicularly upwards. A foul lines are in fair territory.

A FIELDER is any defensive player.

FIELDER'S CHOICE is the act of a fielder who handles a fa grounder and, instead of throwing to first base to put out the batter runner, throws to another base in an attempt to put out a preceding runner. The term is also used by scorers (a) to account for the advance of the batter-runner who takes one or more extra bases whe the fielder who handles his safe hit attempts to put out a preceding runner; (b) to account for the advance of a runner (other than a stolen base or error) while a fielder is attempting to put out anothe runner; and (c) to account for the advance of a runner made sole because of the defensive team's indifference (undefended steal).

A FLY BALL is a batted ball that goes high in the air in flight.

A FORCE PLAY is a play in which a runner legally loses his rig to occupy a base by reason of the batter becoming a runner.

Confusion regarding this play is removed by remembering that the fr quently the "force" situation is removed during the play. Example: Man first, one out, ball hit sharply to first baseman who touches the bag and ba ter-runner is out. The force is removed at that moment and runner advan ing to second must be tagged. If there had been a runner on third or secon and either of these runners scored before the tag-out at second, the r counts. Had the first baseman thrown to second and the ball then had be returned to first, the play at second was a force out, making two outs, and return throw to first ahead of the runner would have made three outs. In th case, no run would score.

Example: Not a force out. One out. Runner on first and third. Batter fl out. Two out. Runner on third tags up and scores. Runner on first tries retouch before throw from fielder reaches first baseman, but does not g back in time and is out. Three outs. If, in umpire's judgment, the runner fr third touched home before the ball was held at first base, the run counts.

A FORFEITED GAME is a game declared ended by the umpi in-chief in favor of the offended team by the score of 9 to 0, for vio tion of the rules.

A FOUL BALL is a batted ball that settles on foul territory tween home and first base, or between home and third base, or th bounds past first or third base on or over foul territory, or that fi falls on foul territory beyond first or third base, or that, while on over foul territory, touches the person of an umpire or player, or a object foreign to the natural ground.

A foul fly shall be judged according to the relative position of the ball and the foul line, including the foul pole, and not as to whether the fielder is on foul or fair territory at the time he touches the ball.

A batted ball not touched by a fielder, which hits the pitcher's rubber a rebounds into foul territory, between home and first, or between home a third base is a foul ball.

FOUL TERRITORY is that part of the playing field outside fl first and third base lines extended to the fence and perpendicular upwards.

A FOUL TIP is a batted ball that goes sharp and direct from th bat to the catcher's hands and is legally caught. It is not a foul unless caught and any foul tip that is caught is a strike, and the ball in play. It is not a catch if it is a rebound, unless the ball has fir touched the catcher's glove or hand.

A GROUND BALL is a batted ball that rolls or bounces close the ground.